W9-CBH-561

I Wonder Why

Trees Have Leaves

and other questions about plants

Andrew Charman

KINGFISHER

BOSTON

KINGFISHER
a Houghton Mifflin Company imprint
222 Berkeley Street
Boston, Massachusetts 02116
www.houghtonmifflinbooks.com

First published in 1997
First published in this format in 2003

10 9 8 7 6 5 4 3 2 1
1TR/0403/SHE/UNV(FR)/126.6MA

Copyright © Kingfisher Publications Plc 1994

All rights reserved under International
and Pan-American Copyright Conventions

LIBRARY OF CONGRESS CATALOGING-IN-PUBLICATION DATA
Charman, Andy.
      I wonder why trees have leaves / Andrew Charman.—
      1st American ed.
            p.   cm. (I wonder why)
      Includes index.
      Summary: Questions and answers explore the world
of plants, covering such aspects as leaves, roots, stems,
seeds, and fruit.
      1. Plants—Miscellanea—Juvenile literature. [1. Plants
—Miscellanea. 2. Questions and answers.] I. Title.
II. Series: I wonder why (New York, N. Y.)
      QK49.C44   1997
      580—dc21   97-189 CIP AC

ISBN 0-7534-5663-X

Printed in Taiwan

Series editor: Claire Oliver
Series designer: David West Children's Books
Consultant: Michael Chinery
Editor: Claire Llewellyn
Art editor: Christina Fraser
Illustrator: All cartoons by Tony Kenyon (B.L. Kearley)

CONTENTS

What is a plant?

Plants are living things. They come in all shapes and sizes, from tiny waterweeds to towering trees. Plants are different from animals in one very important way—they can make food for themselves from sunlight. Animals can't do this. They depend on plants for their food.

Where do plants grow?

There are about 380,000 different kinds of plants on Earth, and they grow just about everywhere —in fields and forests, deserts and mountains. Besides air, the two things plants need are sunlight and water, so you won't find them in places that are completely dark or dry.

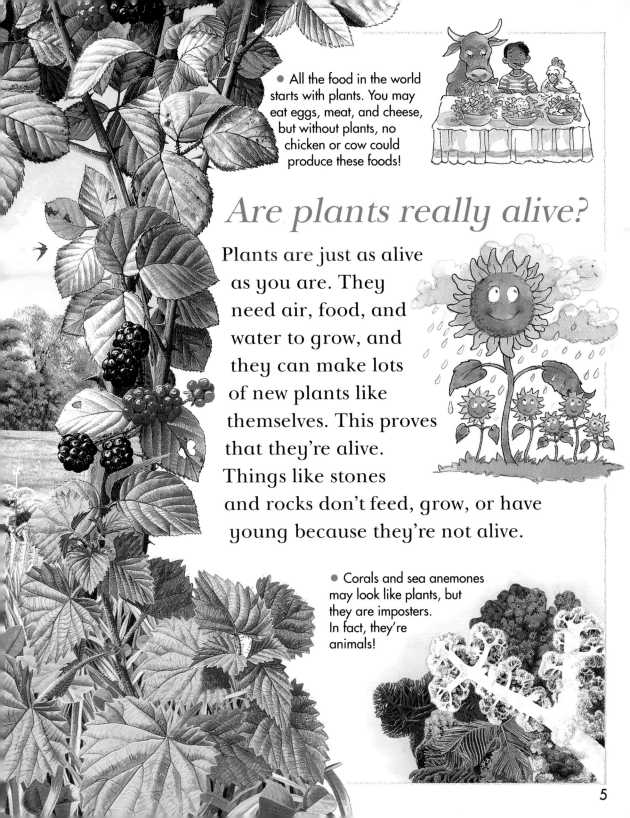

● All the food in the world starts with plants. You may eat eggs, meat, and cheese, but without plants, no chicken or cow could produce these foods!

Are plants really alive?

Plants are just as alive as you are. They need air, food, and water to grow, and they can make lots of new plants like themselves. This proves that they're alive. Things like stones and rocks don't feed, grow, or have young because they're not alive.

● Corals and sea anemones may look like plants, but they are imposters. In fact, they're animals!

Why do trees have leaves?

Like all plants, trees need their leaves to stay alive. Leaves are a tree's food factories. They contain a sticky green substance called chlorophyll. The chlorophyll uses the energy from sunlight to turn water and carbon dioxide into a sugary food. The food is then carried to every part of the tree in a sweet and sticky juice called sap.

● If you've ever chewed a blade of grass, you'll know how sweet sap tastes. Hungry young caterpillars think so too. That's why they eat leaves! Grass and leaves are both full of sap.

Why do some trees lose their leaves in the fall?

Big green leaves are useful in spring and summer. They make food while the sun shines and the days are long. When the days get shorter, there is less time for making food and the tree has to live off of its food reserves. Some trees shed their leaves in the fall so they don't have to feed them, too!

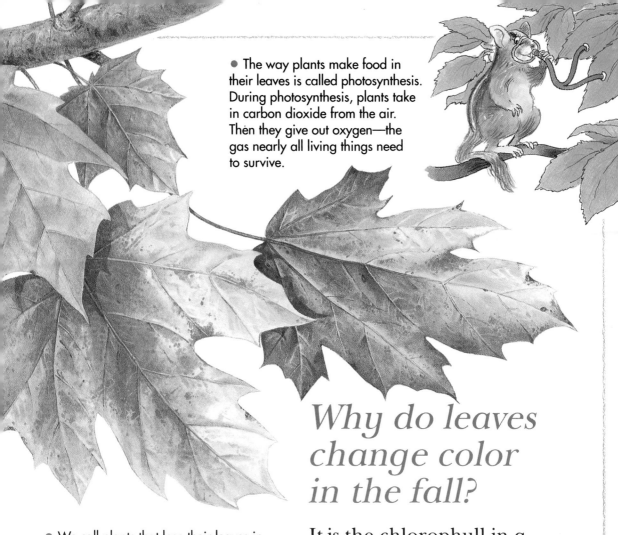

• The way plants make food in their leaves is called photosynthesis. During photosynthesis, plants take in carbon dioxide from the air. Then they give out oxygen—the gas nearly all living things need to survive.

Why do leaves change color in the fall?

• We call plants that lose their leaves in the fall deciduous. Evergreen trees have tough leaves that can survive the winter. Evergreen trees still lose their leaves, but not all at the same time.

It is the chlorophyll in a plant's leaves that makes them look green. But in the fall, the chlorophyll breaks down. When the green coloring has gone, the leaves' other colors show through—beautiful shades of red, yellow, and gold.

Why do roots grow so long?

Long roots keep a plant firmly in the ground so it won't fall over on windy days. But roots do another job, too. By spreading out underground, they can suck up the water and minerals from the soil that the plants need to grow. Then the stems carry the water from the roots up to the leaves.

● In the strongest winds, a tree can sometimes be blown over. Its roots are wrenched out of the ground as the tree falls down with a crash.

● A wild fig tree in South Africa grew roots 400 feet down into the soil. If it was put on the roof of a 40-story office building, its roots would reach down to the ground.

● There are tiny hairs at the ends of the roots. They burrow into the spaces between pebbles and grains of soil.

● Sunflowers not only grow up toward the light, but their flowers also follow the Sun! As the Sun moves across the sky through the day, the flower heads turn to face it.

Why are stems so straight?

A plant needs to hold its leaves up to the sunshine, which it uses to make its food. Many plants grow tall, straight stems so that they can beat their neighbors to the sunlight.

● Not all plants have straight stems. Some have stems that bend and curl, scrambling their way over nearby plants as they climb up to the light.

Which plants grow in water?

The giant water lily grows in the lakes and rivers of South America. Its roots lie deep in the mud and its huge leaves float on the surface of the water. This is the best place for sunbathing! Each leaf curls up at the rim so that it can push other leaves aside.

● The giant water lily's leaves grow on long, strong stems. On the underside of each leaf is a web of supporting veins. This makes the leaves so strong that a small child could sit on one without sinking!

Which are the smallest plants?

Some members of the algae family of plants can grow to be enormous, but others are so small you can only see them through a microscope. The very smallest algae float in lakes and oceans and are called phytoplankton. They're so tiny that a whale can catch millions in a single gulp!

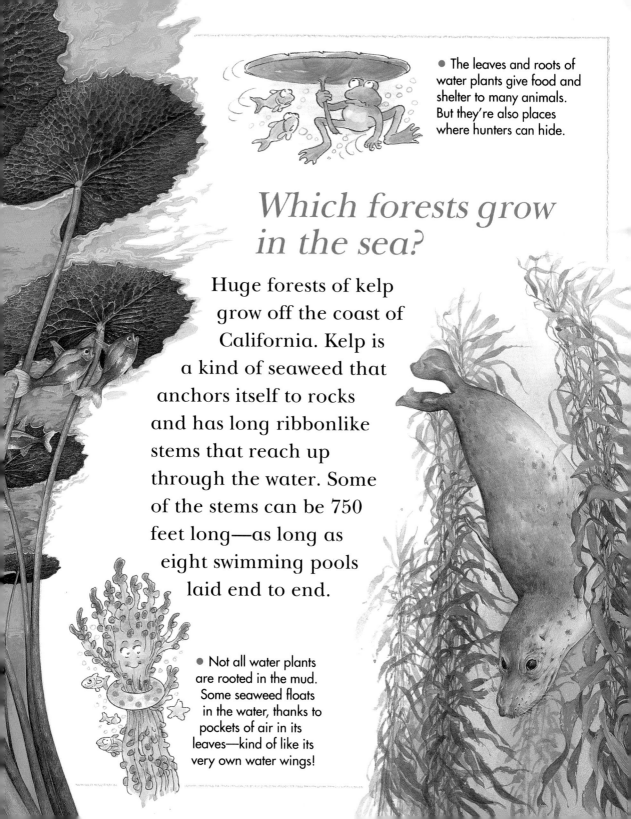

● The leaves and roots of water plants give food and shelter to many animals. But they're also places where hunters can hide.

Which forests grow in the sea?

Huge forests of kelp grow off the coast of California. Kelp is a kind of seaweed that anchors itself to rocks and has long ribbonlike stems that reach up through the water. Some of the stems can be 750 feet long—as long as eight swimming pools laid end to end.

● Not all water plants are rooted in the mud. Some seaweed floats in the water, thanks to pockets of air in its leaves—kind of like its very own water wings!

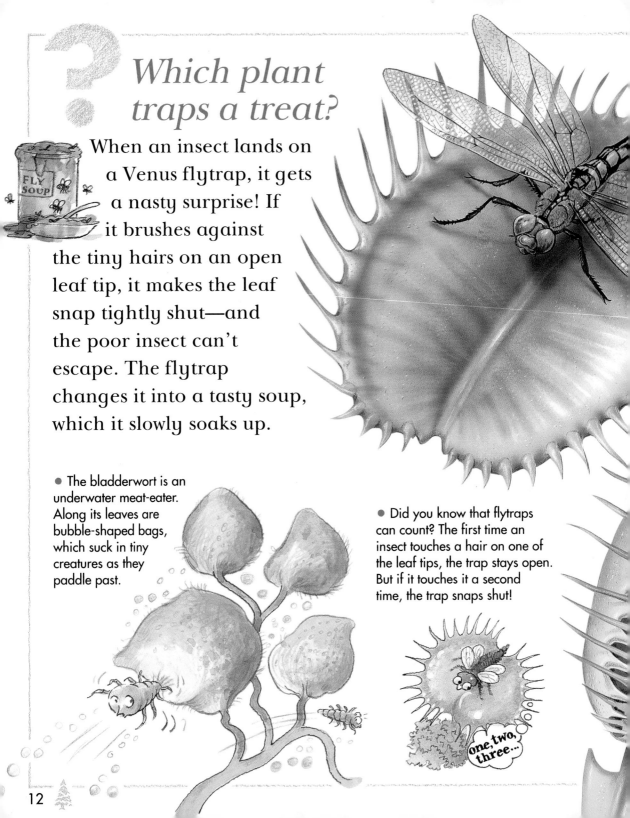

Which plant traps a treat?

When an insect lands on a Venus flytrap, it gets a nasty surprise! If it brushes against the tiny hairs on an open leaf tip, it makes the leaf snap tightly shut—and the poor insect can't escape. The flytrap changes it into a tasty soup, which it slowly soaks up.

FLY SOUP

● The bladderwort is an underwater meat-eater. Along its leaves are bubble-shaped bags, which suck in tiny creatures as they paddle past.

● Did you know that flytraps can count? The first time an insect touches a hair on one of the leaf tips, the trap stays open. But if it touches it a second time, the trap snaps shut!

one, two, three...

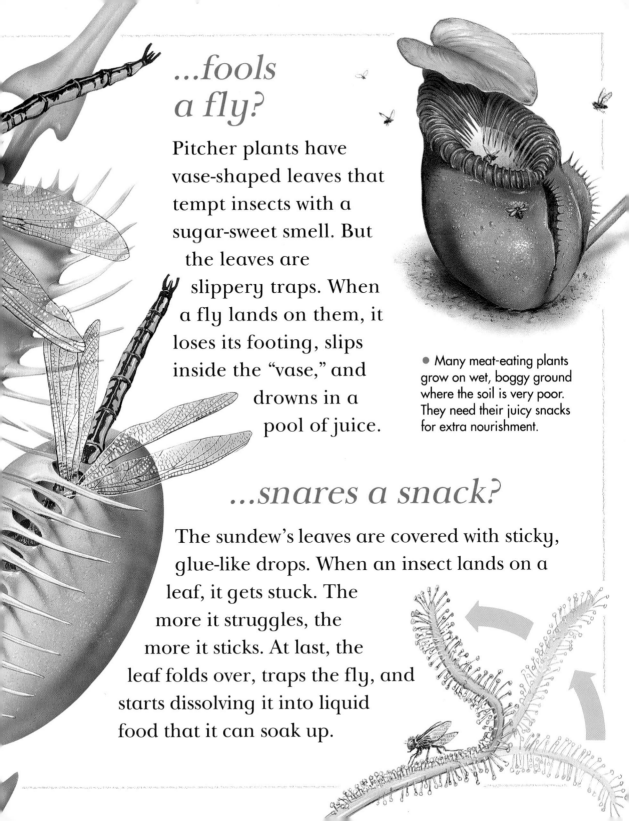

...fools a fly?

Pitcher plants have vase-shaped leaves that tempt insects with a sugar-sweet smell. But the leaves are slippery traps. When a fly lands on them, it loses its footing, slips inside the "vase," and drowns in a pool of juice.

● Many meat-eating plants grow on wet, boggy ground where the soil is very poor. They need their juicy snacks for extra nourishment.

...snares a snack?

The sundew's leaves are covered with sticky, glue-like drops. When an insect lands on a leaf, it gets stuck. The more it struggles, the more it sticks. At last, the leaf folds over, traps the fly, and starts dissolving it into liquid food that it can soak up.

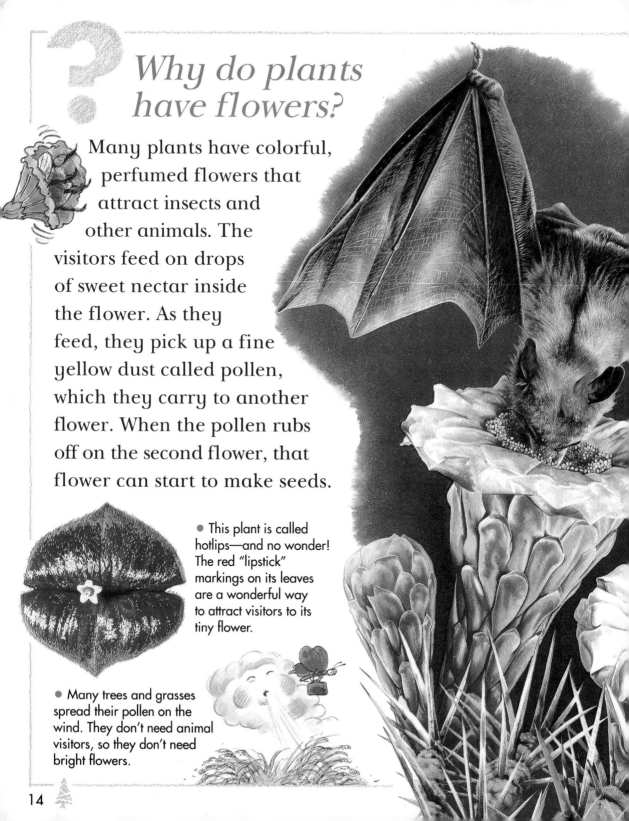

Why do plants have flowers?

Many plants have colorful, perfumed flowers that attract insects and other animals. The visitors feed on drops of sweet nectar inside the flower. As they feed, they pick up a fine yellow dust called pollen, which they carry to another flower. When the pollen rubs off on the second flower, that flower can start to make seeds.

● This plant is called hotlips—and no wonder! The red "lipstick" markings on its leaves are a wonderful way to attract visitors to its tiny flower.

● Many trees and grasses spread their pollen on the wind. They don't need animal visitors, so they don't need bright flowers.

● Pollinators, such as this bat, don't mean to get pollen all over themselves. But a cactus flower is shaped in such a way that the bat just can't help it!

Which flower fools a bee?

A bee orchid's flowers look and smell just like female bees. Male bees zoom to the flowers wanting to mate with them—but they've been tricked! The plant is just using them as mailmen to deliver little packages of pollen to other orchids nearby.

● During the summer, the air can be so full of pollen that it makes many people sneeze. Poor things—they don't have a cold, they have hayfever.

Which is the smelliest flower?

The dead horse arum is well named—it stinks of rotten meat! But blowflies love it. These plump flies usually lay their eggs inside the rotting bodies of dead animals. They're fooled by the plant's rotten smell and crawl inside it to lay their eggs, picking up pollen on the way.

Why is fruit so sweet and juicy?

● The cotton-top tamarin lives in the South American rain forest. It feeds mainly on fruit, especially delicious, juicy figs.

Plants make sweet, juicy fruits so that animals will eat them. Inside every fruit is one or more seeds. When an animal swallows the fruit, it swallows the seeds, too. These pass through its body and fall out in the animal's droppings. In such good soil, the seeds soon start to grow into new plants!

● You often see seeds floating through the air. Dandelion seeds grow their own fluffy parachutes. And maple tree seeds have wings, which spin them to the ground like tiny helicopters.

Which plant shoots from the hip?

The Mediterranean squirting cucumber has a special way of spreading its seeds. As the fruit grows, it fills with a slimy juice. Day by day, the fruit grows fuller and fuller until it bursts, flinging the seeds out into the air.

Which seeds sail away?

Coconut palms grow near the shore, so the ripe coconuts often fall into the water. Protected by their hard shells, they float out to sea. After several weeks or months, they are washed up on to a beach, where they sprout and start to grow.

● Fruits come in many different colors, but most animals seem to like red ones the best!

Which fruit gets forgotten?

Many animals feed on acorns, the fruits of the oak tree. Squirrels enjoy them so much that every fall they bury some in the ground as a snack for when food is scarce in winter. The trouble is, the squirrels often forget where they've hidden their store, so when spring comes the young oaks start to grow.

When does a seed begin to grow?

Inside every seed is the tiny beginning of a new plant. This starts to grow when the soil around the seed is warm and damp. At first, the baby plant feeds on the food stored inside the seed. But as soon as its first leaves open, it begins to make food for itself.

- The seed of the horse-chestnut tree has a tough brown coat. This rots away in the winter, and the young plant bursts through in the spring.

1 The bean seed swells with water and splits open. A root starts to grow.

2 Tiny hairs grow out from the branches of the root.

3 A shoot appears. It grows up toward the light.

Do all plants grow from seeds?

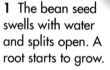

Strawberry plants don't need seeds to produce new plants. They can send out side shoots, called runners. Where these touch the ground, roots begin to grow, then leaves and stems. In just a few weeks, there's a brand new plant!

- The coco-de-mer palm tree grows the largest seeds. They weigh 45 pounds—as much as a sack of potatoes.

Which plant grows the fastest?

The bamboo plant is the fastest-growing plant in the world. Some kinds can grow nearly three feet a day. At that rate, they'd reach the roof of a two-story house in a single week!

4 The shoot grows leaves. Now the new bean plant can make food for itself.

- A cycad tree in Mexico must hold the record as the world's slowest-growing plant. After 120 years, it was only 4 inches high!

Are fungi plants?

Fungi aren't really plants at all. They look like plants, and they grow in the same sort of places. But unlike plants, they don't have leaves, stems, or roots, and they don't make their food from sunlight. A fungus grows by soaking up food from dead animals and plants.

● Scientists have found over 100,000 different kinds of fungi—and there are probably many more. These bright blue toadstools grow in New Zealand.

What puffs out of a puffball?

A puffball is a kind of fungus that looks like a large creamy ball. If you knock a ripe one, a huge cloud of dust puffs out of the top. This dust is really millions of tiny specks called spores. Spores do the same job as seeds. If they land in rich soil, they will grow into brand new puffballs.

- Did you know that the blue veins in some cheeses are a kind of fungus?

- There were plants on land long before there were animals. Some of the types that plant-eating dinosaurs ate are still around today.

Which are the oldest plants?

Soft mosses and tall ferns first appeared on land about 350 million years ago. But the very first plants appeared on Earth more than three billion years earlier. They were tiny, microscopic plants called algae, which floated in the sea.

- One kind of fungus not only feeds on dead animals, it kills them first! The tiny spores grow inside live ants, feeding on the juicy bits of their bodies. Soon, nothing is left but the ant's dry skeleton, with the toadstools growing out of it.

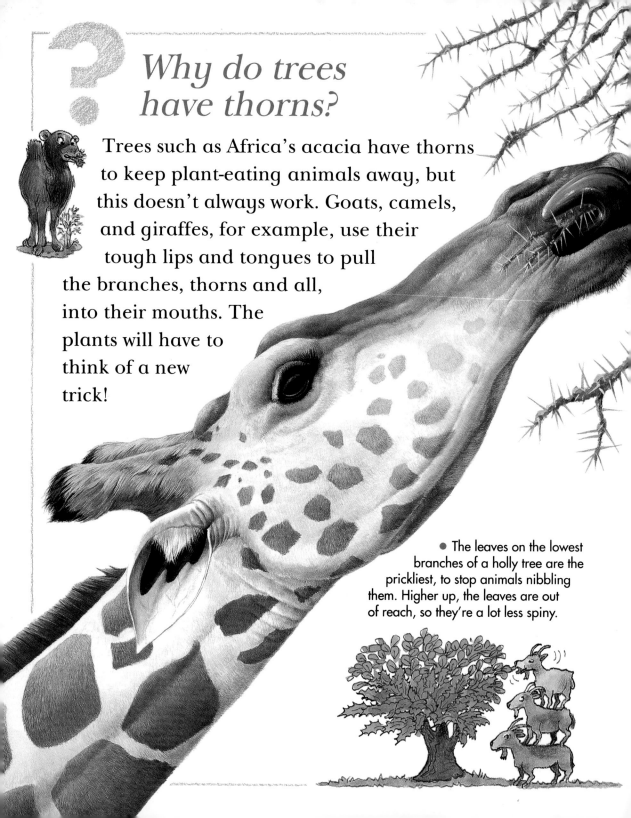

Why do trees have thorns?

Trees such as Africa's acacia have thorns to keep plant-eating animals away, but this doesn't always work. Goats, camels, and giraffes, for example, use their tough lips and tongues to pull the branches, thorns and all, into their mouths. The plants will have to think of a new trick!

● The leaves on the lowest branches of a holly tree are the prickliest, to stop animals nibbling them. Higher up, the leaves are out of reach, so they're a lot less spiny.

Why do stinging nettles sting?

Stinging is another way plants protect themselves. Each leaf on a nettle is covered with little hairs as sharp as glass. If an animal touches one, the hair pricks the animal and injects a drop of painful poison— ouch! It won't stick around to eat that leaf!

Which plants look like pebbles?

● Milkweed is a poisonous plant, but the caterpillars of the monarch butterfly can eat it safely. It even makes them poisonous—so they don't get eaten by birds.

Pebble plants grow in the desert in southern Africa. They have two fat, juicy leaves that any animal would love to eat. But the plant protects itself by blending in with the background. Its leaves are disguised to look so much like pebbles that animals ignore it.

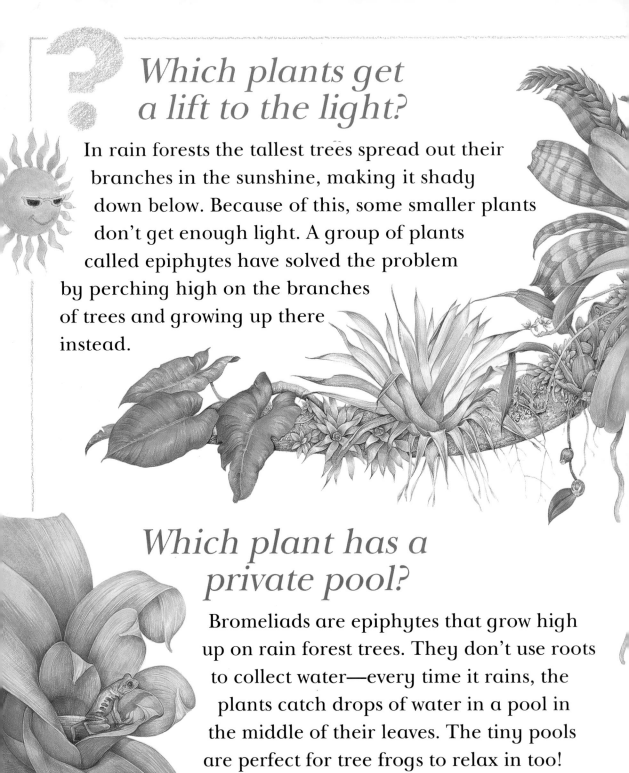

Which plants get a lift to the light?

In rain forests the tallest trees spread out their branches in the sunshine, making it shady down below. Because of this, some smaller plants don't get enough light. A group of plants called epiphytes have solved the problem by perching high on the branches of trees and growing up there instead.

Which plant has a private pool?

Bromeliads are epiphytes that grow high up on rain forest trees. They don't use roots to collect water—every time it rains, the plants catch drops of water in a pool in the middle of their leaves. The tiny pools are perfect for tree frogs to relax in too!

● It's so wet in a rain forest that many plants have leaves with downward-pointing tips. They're like drainpipes for the rain to run down.

● Lianas are climbing plants that dangle from rain forest trees. Some animals use them as ropes and swing on them through the trees.

● Not all epiphytes collect water in their leaves. Some, such as orchids, have long trailing roots, which soak up water from the humid air like a sponge.

Which plants strangle and squeeze?

The strangler fig is well-named because it strangles other trees to death! Its seed sprouts high up on the branch of a tree. Week by week, its roots grow longer—wrapping around the branches, down the trunk, and into the ground. The fig now sucks all the goodness out of the soil, starving its host until it dies.

Can plants grow in a desert?

Plants can grow in a desert, but they need special ways to survive. Cacti have spreading roots that soak up any rain as soon as it falls. Then they take great care of the water, storing it inside their fat, juicy stems. It may have to last them weeks, months, or even years.

● Desert plants save lives! Many thirsty travelers have sucked life-saving water from the juicy flesh of a cactus.

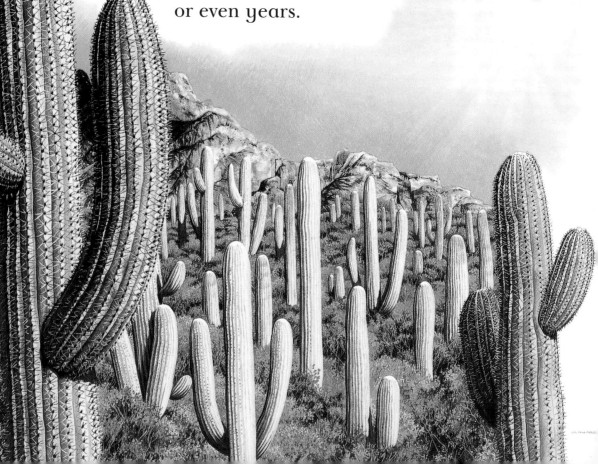

Can you pick fruit in the desert?

People have been picking bunches of sweet, sticky dates in Africa and the Middle East for more than 5,000 years. Today, this delicious fruit can be found dangling from palm trees in the deserts of other countries, too.

FOR SALE

● A gila woodpecker makes a cool nest for itself by carving out a hole in a cactus. When it leaves, there's a long line of other birds who'd like to move in!

Can you find flowers in the desert?

Daisies, poppies, cacti, and many other plants flower in the desert. The plants wither and die during the hot, dry months, but their seeds survive in the ground. When it rains, they quickly spring into action. They grow into new plants and cover the dry desert with a beautiful carpet of flowers within a few weeks.

Which are the tastiest plants?

Spices are made from plants. They have such a delicious smell and taste that we use them in cooking to add flavor to food. After being harvested, most spices are dried and then crushed to a powder that you can add to your food.

● Spices are made from different parts of plants. Pepper comes from berries, cinnamon from bark, and ginger from a root.

● Most spices come from plants that grow in tropical parts of the world. For hundreds of years, merchants have traveled around the world to buy spices at markets like this.

Why do carrot plants grow carrots?

A carrot is a tasty food—but it's not really meant for us! Carrot plants live for just two years. In the first year they make food, which they store in a fat orange root. They use up the food in the second year, while they're growing flowers and seeds—as long as the carrots haven't already been picked!

• Roots, berries, leaves, and seeds—plants give us so many wonderful foods that some people eat no meat at all. They are called vegetarians.

Do people ever eat grass?

Wheat, rice, corn, barley, oats, and rye are just some of the grasses that people eat all over the world. We don't eat the leaves like cows and other animals do. We harvest the seeds. Then we either eat them whole or grind them into flour to make bread, pasta, and other important foods.

• Scientists can improve seeds so that they grow into stronger, healthier plants. This helps farmers to grow bigger and better crops.

What are 300-million-year-old plants good for?

Three hundred million years ago, there were huge forests of trees and ferns. As the plants died, they fell into muddy swamps and were buried in the mud. Slowly, over millions of years, the plants were pressed down and turned into a black rock called coal. Coal is a fuel. We burn it in power plants to make electricity.

● The coal we burn today comes from plants that grew before there were even dinosaurs!

● Shampoos, perfumes, bath oils, and creams are all made from sweet-smelling plants. That's how you smell so sweet!

● In some parts of the world, people run their cars on fuels made from corn, potato, and sugarcane plants.

• The corks that seal bottles of wine are made from the bark of the cork oak tree.

• Many of the medicines we buy at the drugstore are made from plants.

PHARMACIST

What are plants good for today?

Today's plants are still giving us the food and oxygen we need to survive. They also help us to make lots of useful things, such as paper, clothes, and medicines. Every year, scientists discover new plants and new ways to use them.

• All sorts of useful things are made from rubber. It comes from the sticky juices of the rubber tree.

Cotton

Flax

• Cotton cloth is made from the soft hairs that surround the cotton plant's seeds. Linen is made from the stems of the flax plant.

Index